MINECRAFTERS FUN MATHS

VERSION 1.0

PhD. Felipe García Gaitero

Copyright © 2023 PhD. Felipe García Gaitero

All rights reserved.
No part of this publication may be reproduced, distributed, or transmitted in any form or by any means, including photocopying, recording, or other electronic or mechanical methods, without the prior written permission of the author.

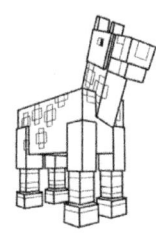

INDEX

BASIC LEVEL

The Island of Mushrooms	Problem solving	8
Alex's new Armour	Additions and subtractions	9
Counting Blocks	Additions	10
Steve has a sweet tooth	Pictograms	11
Blocks Sequence	Number sequence	12
Flower Bouquets	Problem solving	13
Creepers Attack	Subtractions	14
Counting my Little Animals	Bar Charts	15
Carrot Harvest	Additions and subtractions	16
Bitcoin Mine	Additions	17
Master Armorer	Problem solving	18
Coordinates X Y	Coordinates	19
Secret Code	Coordinates	20
Deactivating TNT	Numerical operations	21

INTERMEDIATE LEVEL

Ocelots in the Jungle	Problem solving	24
The Ocelot's Life	Fractions	25
The Black Sheep	Problem solving	26
Crafting with Iron	Division	27
The day's Schedule	Hours	28
Wheat, Bread and Coockies	Division, subtraction, fractions	29
Bread and Fish	Grouping, additions	30
Blocks Sequence V2	Symbolic sequences	31
The Dolphyn's Chest	Square numbers	32
Divide and Conquer	Problem solving	33
Tasks of the Day	Porportionality	34
My own Castle	Data handling	35
The Passage of Time	Time	36

INDEX

AVANCED LEVEL

Tom's Little House	Area and perimeter	38
Food Bank	Porportionality	39
The Vegetable Garden	Area and perimeter	40
Counting Animals	Data handling and percentajes	41
False Redstone	Problem solving	42
Watering Lands	Division, percentaje	43
The Spiders Attack	Percentaje, proportionality	44
Alex the Architect	Data handling and percentajes	45

BASIC LEVEL

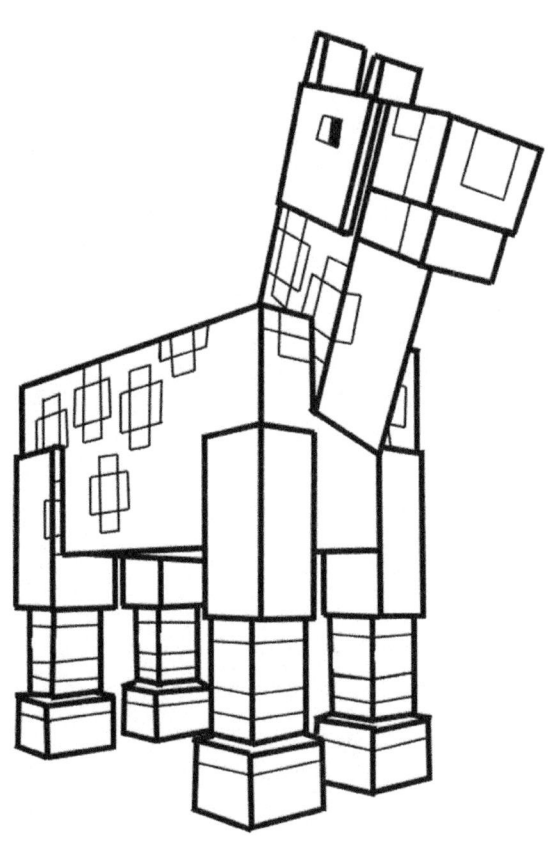

BASIC ⫶ PROBLEM SOLVING

THE ISLAND OF MUSHROOMS

In one of his journeys towards the desert, Steve discovers an island where red and brown mushrooms grow and decides to gather several to store them in his inventory.

1. After visiting the island, Steve has amassed an inventory of 15 mushrooms, of which 8 are brown. How many red mushrooms does he have?

Answer: _____

2. Two days later, Steve feels peckish and decides to make soup with the mushrooms he gathered on the island. To make a mushroom soup, one requires 1 red mushroom and 1 brown mushroom. How many mushroom soup can Steve prepare?

Answer: _____

3. After preparing the mushroom soup, Steve decides to consume 3. We know that for each mushroom soup, 3 points of hunger are restored. How many hunger points does Steve recover?

Answer: _____

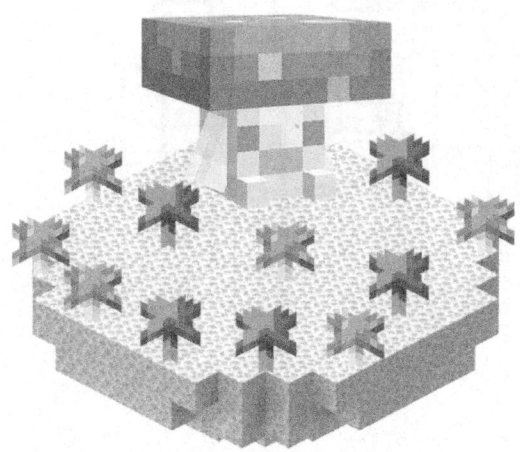

ALEX'S NEW ARMOR

Alex wishes to spend the diamonds from his inventory to purchase armor to protect himself from the onslaught of the zombies.

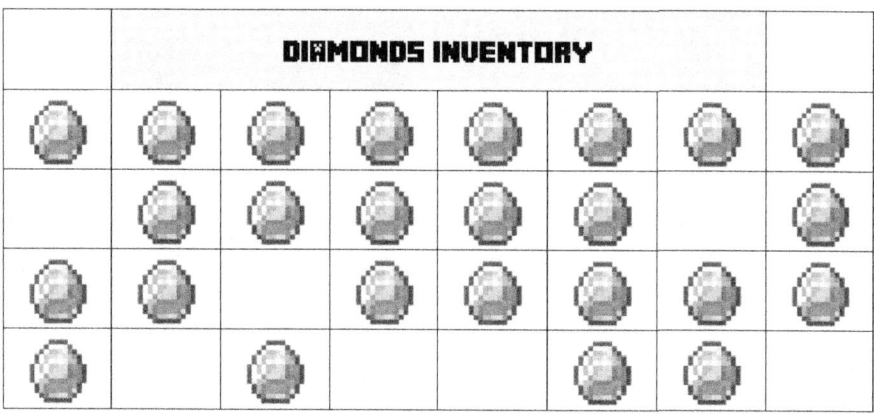

1. How many diamonds are there in the inventory?

Answer: _____

2. If I purchase all the armor parts except the helmet, how many emeralds are left over?

Answer: _____

BASIC || ADDITIONS

COUNTING BLOCKS

To become expert players in Minecraft, we must be agile in counting blocks. Help Alex to count the blocks in each of the following groups:

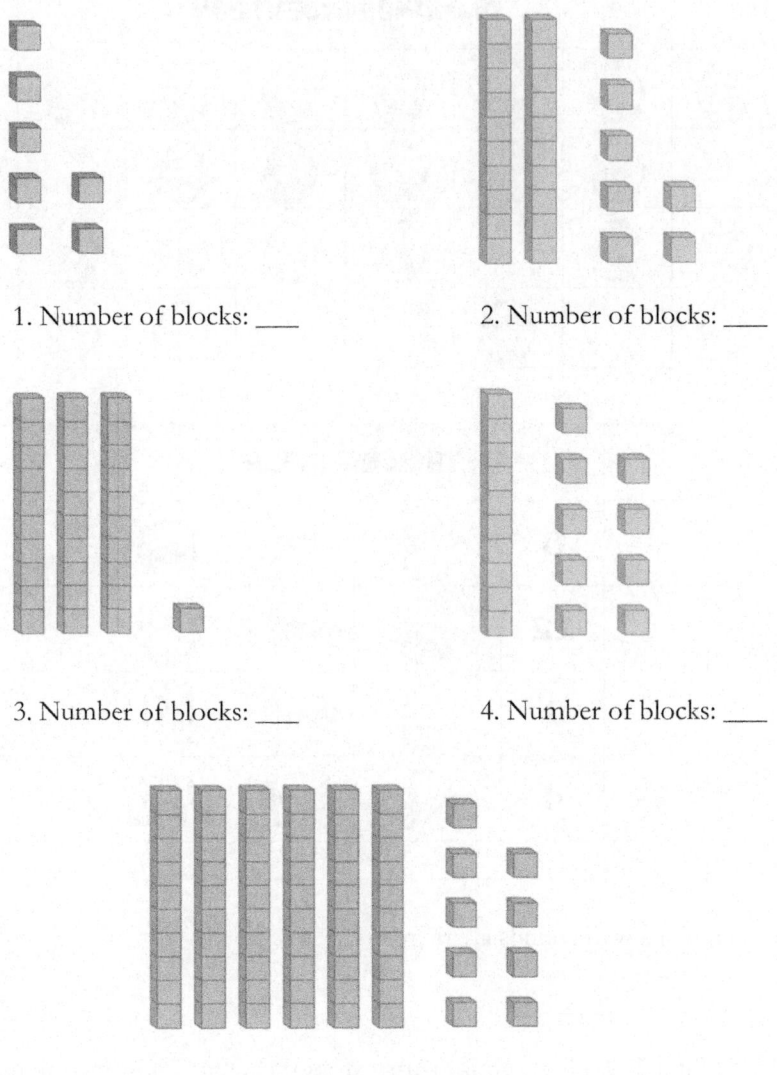

1. Number of blocks: ___

2. Number of blocks: ___

3. Number of blocks: ___

4. Number of blocks: ___

5. Number of blocks: ___

BASIC || PICTOGRAMS

STEVE HAS A SWEET TOOTH

Steve is very fond of sweets; he could spend the entire day munching on cookies, cakes, and pastries non-stop. Lately, some creatures have developed quite a sweet tooth as well, so he has decided to hide all the cakes inside 4 chests.

CHEST	NUMBER OF CAKES
1	🎂 🎂
2	🎂 🎂 🎂 🎂 🎂 🎂 🎂
3	🎂 🎂 🎂 🎂 🎂
4	🎂 🎂 🎂

1. How many cakes are there in chest 2?

Answer: _____

2. How many more cakes are there in chest 3 than in chest 1?

Answer: _____

3. How many cakes are there in total stored in the even-numbered chests?

Answer: _____

4. How many cakes does Steve have stored in all the chests?

Answer: _____

BASIC ‖ NUMBER SEQUENCE

BLOCK SEQUENCE

Help Alex to complete the missing numbers.

SEQUENCE 1

		6		10	12	
16		20			26	

SEQUENCE 2

6	9			18	21	
	30		36			45

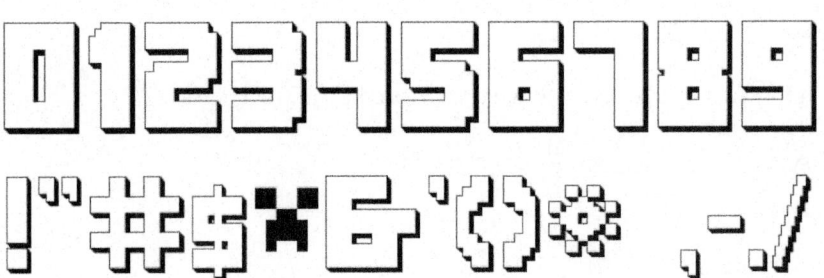

BASIC ‖ EVEN AND ODD

FLOWER BOUQUETS

We have to make 3 bouquets of flowers. The first two bouquets should contain an odd number of flowers each. The third bouquet must have an even number of flowers. Take your time to think about how you are going to arrange the bouquets, and then draw them by encircling the flowers with a pencil. (There are several solutions)

BASIC ‖ SUBTRACTION

CREEPERS ATTACK

There is a total of 13 creepers quietly approaching the house. In the picture, we can only see a few. How many creepers are hidden from our view behind the house?

Answer: _____

BASIC II BAR CHARTS

COUNTING MY LITTLE ANIMALS

The farm is full of animals, and Steve needs to take inventory to know how many he has. In the following chart, you can see the number of pigs, chickens, donkeys, and horses that are in the farm.

ANIMALS IN THE FARM

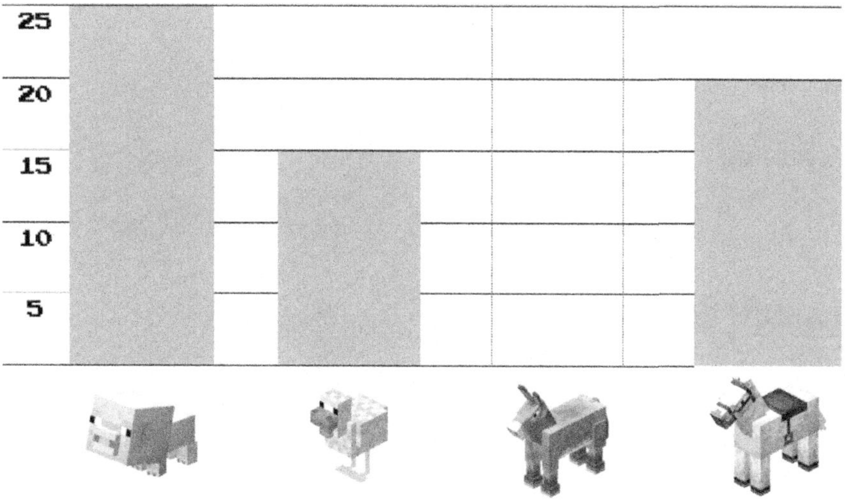

1. How many animals have 2 legs?

Answer: _____

2. There are half as many donkeys as horses on the farm. Draw the number of donkeys on the chart.

Answer: _____

3. How many animals have 4 legs?

Answer: _____

4. How many animals are there in total in the farm?

Answer: _____

BASIC ADDITIONS AND SUBTRACTIONS

CARROT HARVEST

The table below shows the carrot harvest that Molly has carried out over 6 days, from Monday to Saturday.

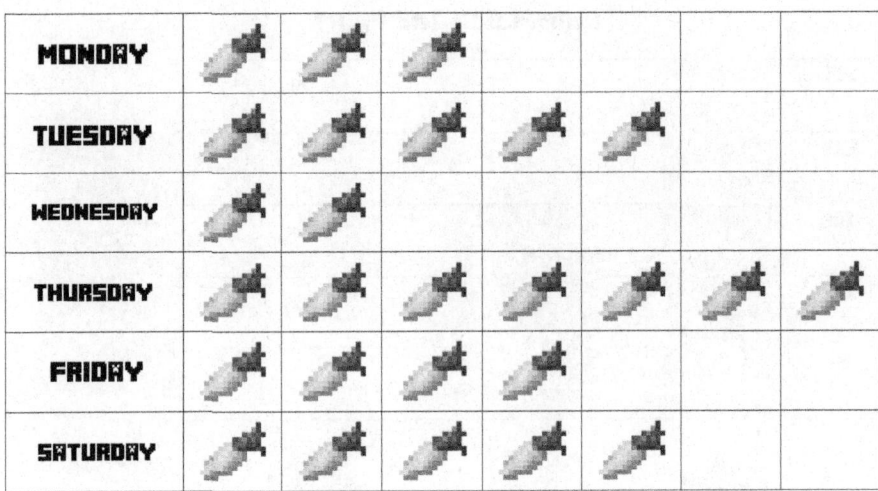

1. On which day were the fewest carrots harvested?

Answer: _____

2. How many carrots have been harvested from Tuesday to Thursday?

Answer: _____

3. How many carrots have been harvested in total?

Answer: _____

4. What is the difference in the number of carrots between the day with the most harvested and the day with the least?

Answer: _____

BASIC :: ADDITIONS AND SUBTRACTIONS

BITCOIN MINE

Ray has discovered a deposit of bitcoins inside the labyrinth mine. To be able to mine and progress to the bitcoin, you must add up all the numbers in the path from the entrance arrow to the center.

What is the sum of all the numbers in the path?

Answer: _____

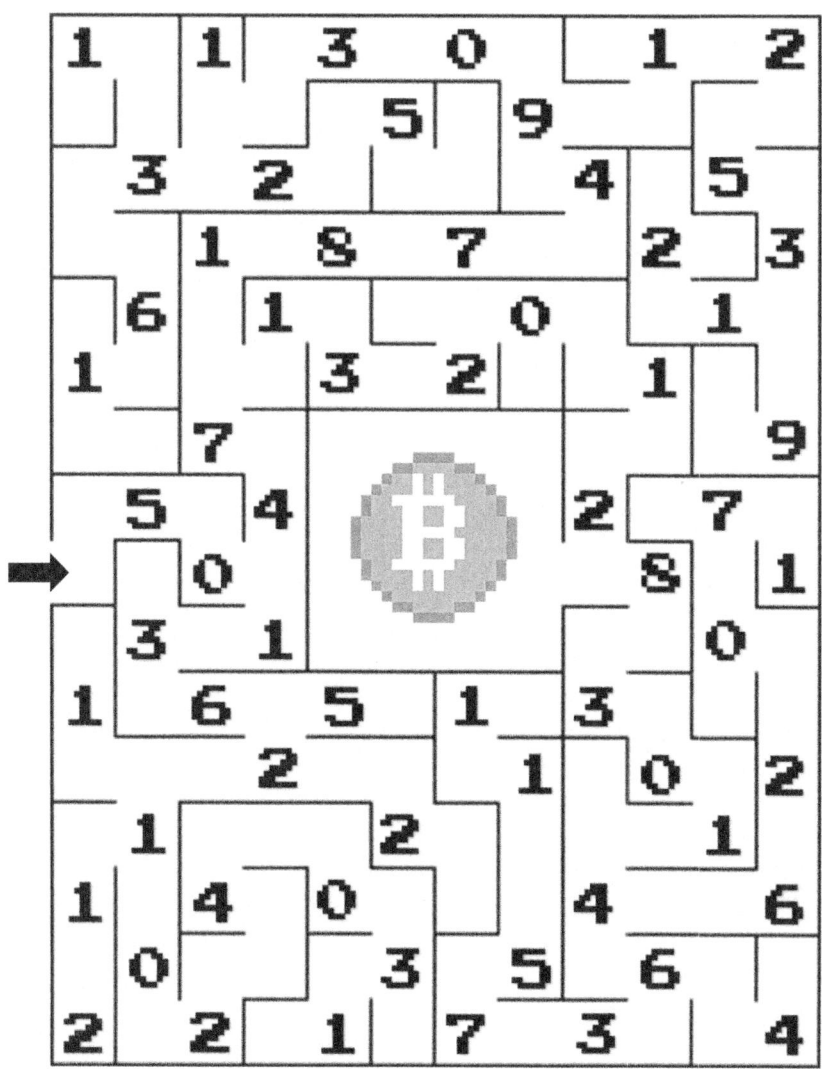

BASIC ‖ PROBLEM SOLVING

MASTER ARMORER

Steve has visited the armorer's house to buy 2 tools. He has spent a total of 18 emeralds.

1. What are the 2 tools that Steve has bought?

Answer: _____

2. In a month, when Steve has saved 22 emeralds, which 3 tools will he be able to buy?

Answer: _____

BASIC ‖ COORDINATES

COORDINATES X Y

Write down the coordinates where each of these objects is located.

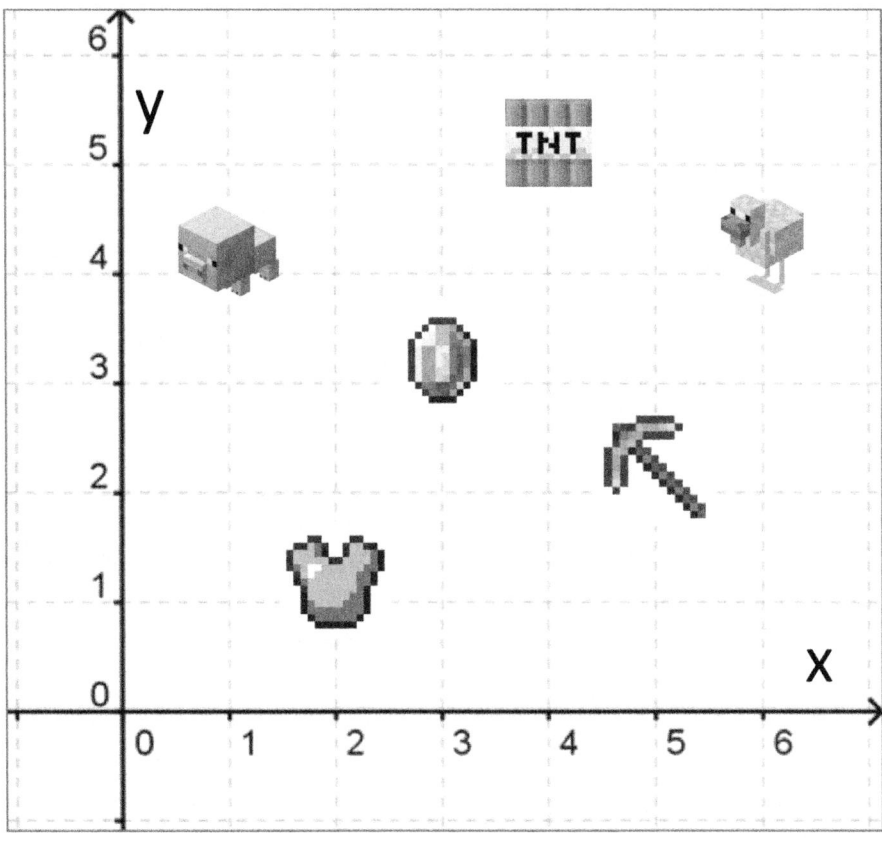

1. Pickaxe: (,) 2. Pig: (,)

3. Chicken: (,) 4. TNT: (,)

5. Emerald: (,) 6. Chestplate: (,)

BASIC II COORDINATES

SECRET CODE

Alex has found a cryptobook hidden inside a box. Use the cryptobook to decipher the food that the villager conceals in the pantry of his house.

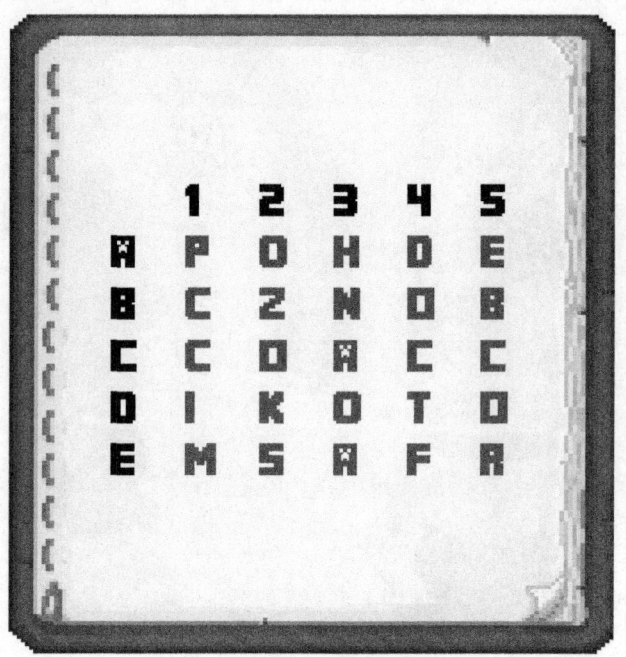

1. 1B, 2A, 3D, 2D, 1D, 5A

Answer: _____

2. 5B, 5E, 5A, 3E, 4A

Answer: _____

3. 1E, 5A, 3C, 4D

Answer: _____

4. 4E, 1D, 2E, 3A

Answer: _____

BASIC ∥ NUMERICAL OPERATIONS

DEACTIVATING TNT

We need to deactivate all the TNT blocks to prevent them from exploding. To do this, we have to write in the center of the block the operator (addition, subtraction, multiplication, or division) that results in the number beneath the arrow.

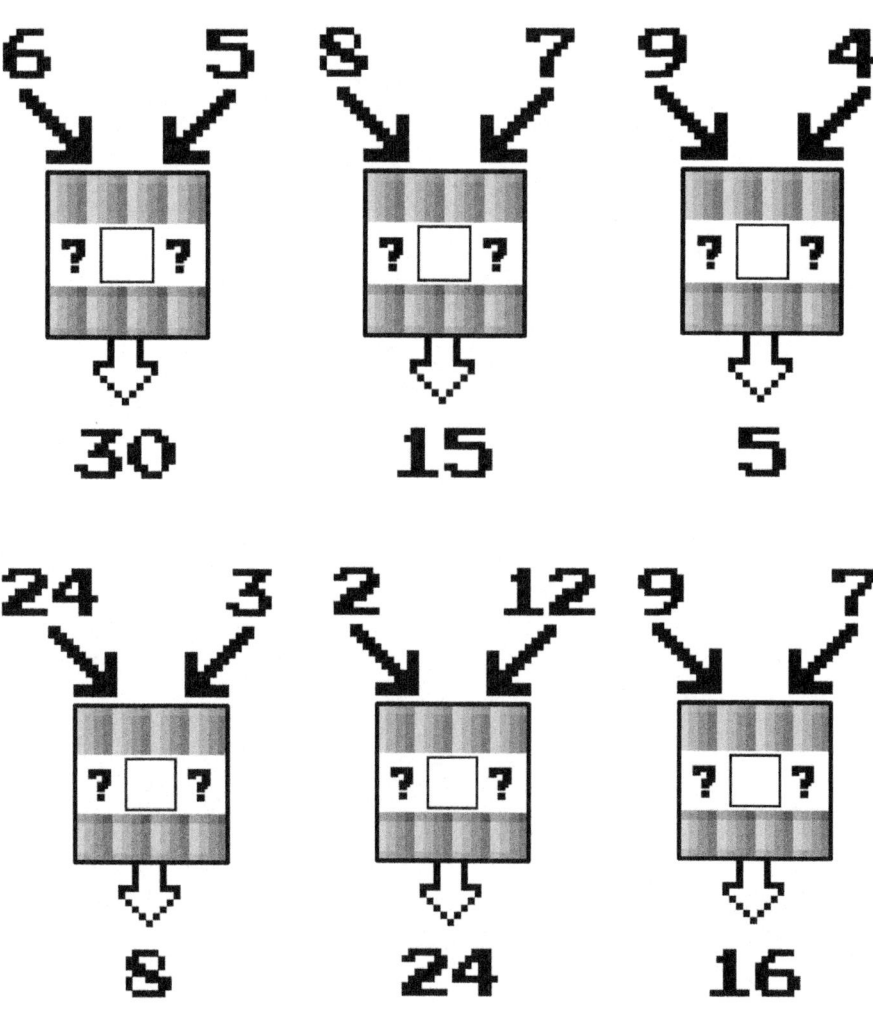

INTERMEDIATE LEVEL

INTERMEDIATE ‖ PROBLEM SOLVING

OCELOTS IN THE JUNGLE

After fishing 20 pieces of raw salmon in the river, Steve explores the jungle in search of ocelots to tame. Steve uses half of the salmon and manages to tame 7 ocelots.

1. How many pieces of raw salmon has Steve used?

Answer: _____

2. When he returns to the village, Steve brings together the ocelots caught in the jungle with 2 more that he had at home. How many ocelots does he have in total?

Answer: _____

3. To feed all the ocelots, Steve gives one piece of raw salmon to each of them. How many pieces of salmon does he have left in the end?

Answer: _____

4. One night, a group of 6 creepers approach Steve's house. After seeing the ocelots, half of the creepers get scared and run away. How many creepers are left near Steve's house?

Answer: _____

INTERMEDIATE ⅠⅠ FRACTIONS

THE OCELOT'S LIFE

1. Baby ocelots that eat raw fish grow faster than the rest. In a population of 90 ocelots, half (1/2) have never eaten fish when they were young. How many ocelots does that make?

Answer: _____

2. In a population of 60 ocelots, one third (1/3) have spawned naturally in the world and live in the jungle. How many ocelots live in the jungle?

Answer: _____

3. We know that a quarter (1/4) of the baby ocelots spawn alongside an adult. If there are 120 adult ocelots in a world, how many babies have spawned?

Answer: _____

4. An adult ocelot attacked a farm with 80 chickens and managed to catch a fifth (1/5) of them. How many chickens escaped the ocelot's attack?

Answer: _____

INTERMEDIATE | PROBLEM SOLVING

THE BLACK SHEEP

1. Steve takes care of 23 sheep in the farm, which come in three different colors. 11 sheep are white and 4 are black. How many sheep are pink?

   Answer: _____

2. There are 2 sheep that are Steve's favorites. One is named Dolly and the other is Molly. Dolly has 4 health points and Molly has twice as much. What is Molly's health level?

   Answer: _____

3. The black sheep has jumped over the fence and run away at a speed of 6 blocks per second. How many blocks will the sheep have traveled in 4 seconds?

   Answer: _____

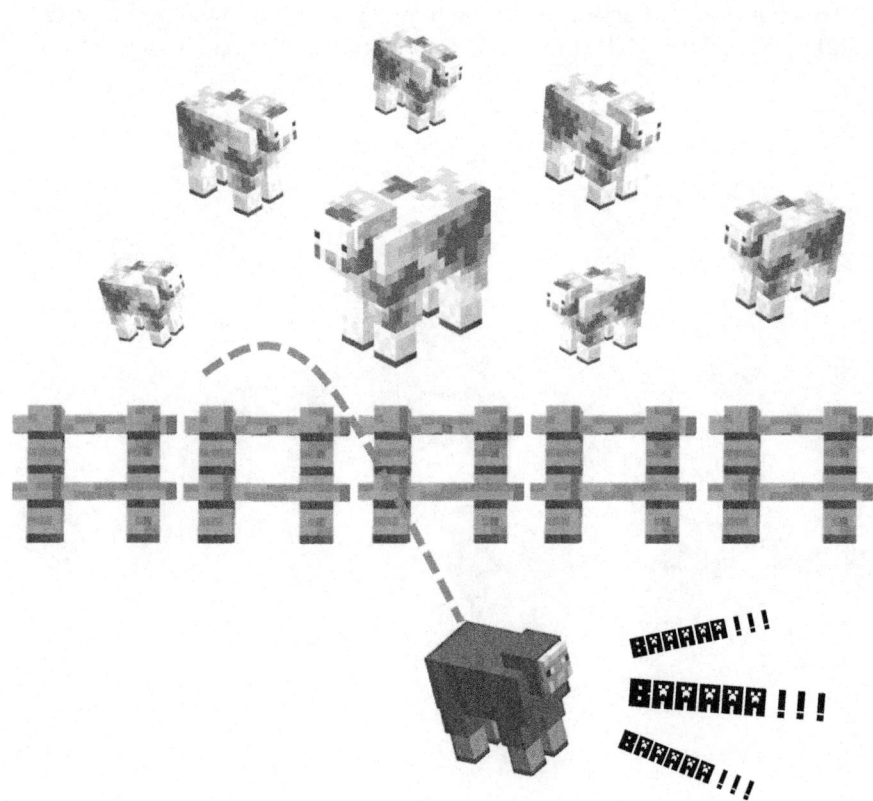

INTERMEDIATE ⅠⅠ DIVISION

CRAFTING WITH IRON

Below are the crafting recipes to craft each part of an iron armor set.

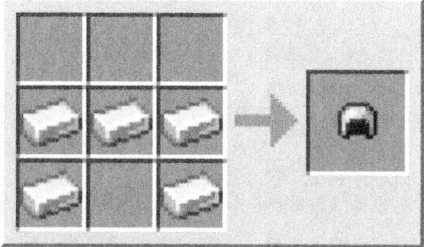
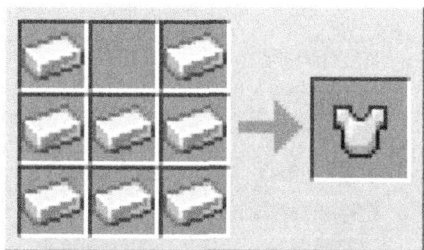
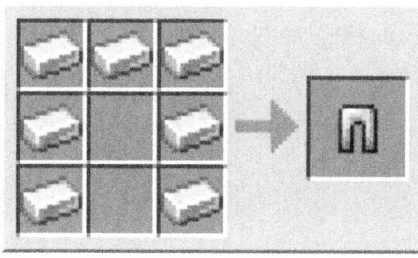
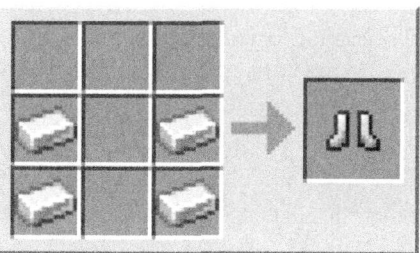

In the inventory, we have a total of 40 iron ingots. What is the maximum quantity of each armor piece that we can craft?

 Num. of helmets: ___

 Num. of chestplates: ___

 Num. of boots: ___

 Num. of chainmails: ___

INTERMEDIATE | HOURS

THE DAY'S SCHEDULE

Phil has logged the amount of time he has spent on various activities while playing Minecraft. Help him complete the missing gaps in the following table.

ACTIVITY	START HOUR	END HOUR	DURATION
MINING	07:00 A.M	07:30 A.M	30 MIN
FARMING	07:30 A.M	07:50 A.M	__ MIN
MELTING	07:50 A.M	__:__ A.M	50 MIN
CRAFTING	__:__ A.M	09:15 A.M	35 MIN
COMBAT	09:15 A.M	10:00 A.M	__ MIN

Use the information from the table to answer the following questions:

1. Which activity ends at 07:50 a.m?

Answer: _____

2. Which activity lasts the shortest amount of time?

Answer: _____

3. Which activity lasts the longest?

Answer: _____

4. How much total time has Phil spent playing Minecraft?

Answer: _____

INTERMEDIATE ∎ **DIVISION. SUBTRACTION. FRACTIONS**

WHEAT, BREAD, AND COOKIES

Steve wants to make bread and cookies to give to his best friends at his birthday party. To do this, he has decided to spend the following items:

9 bales of wheat   **5 pieces of cocoa**

Review the following conversions and elaborations before answering the questions.

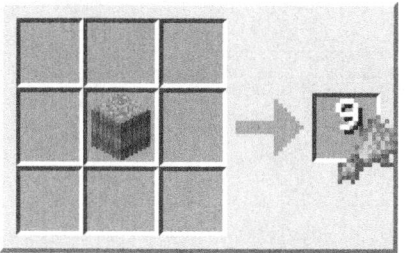
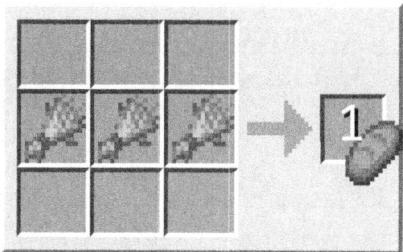
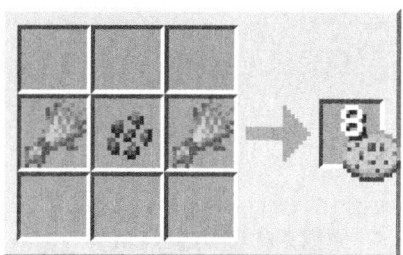

1. First, Steve converts the bales of wheat into wheat spikes. How many wheat spikes does he have in total? _____

2. Next, he spends the 5 pieces of cocoa along with the necessary spikes to make cookies. How many cookies does he make? _____

3. After making the cookies, Steve spends all the remaining spikes on making bread. How many loaves of bread has he made? _____

4. At the end of the entire process, are there any loose spikes left? _____

INTERMEDIATE || GROUPING. ADDITION

BREAD AND FISH

We form groups of 10 to help Steve count the food items he has in his inventory. We know that 10 food items make up 1 decade. The food items that remain after forming the groups are the units.

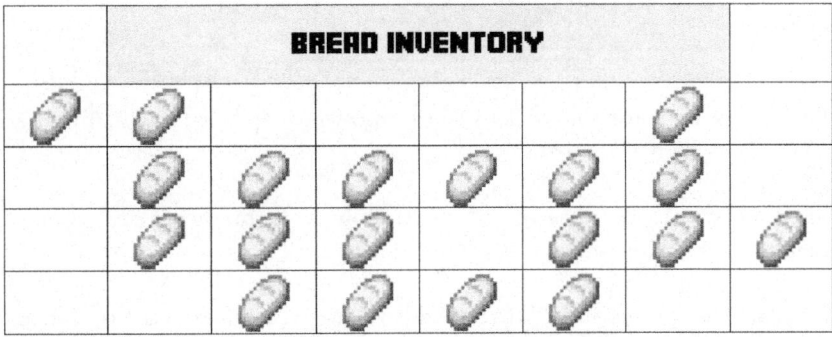

Complete: ☐ tens + ☐ units = ☐

Complete: ☐ tens + ☐ units = ☐

INTERMEDIATE ‖ SYMBOLIC SEQUENCES

BLOCKS SEQUENCE V2

Draw the missing icons in the white cubes to complete the sequence of each line.

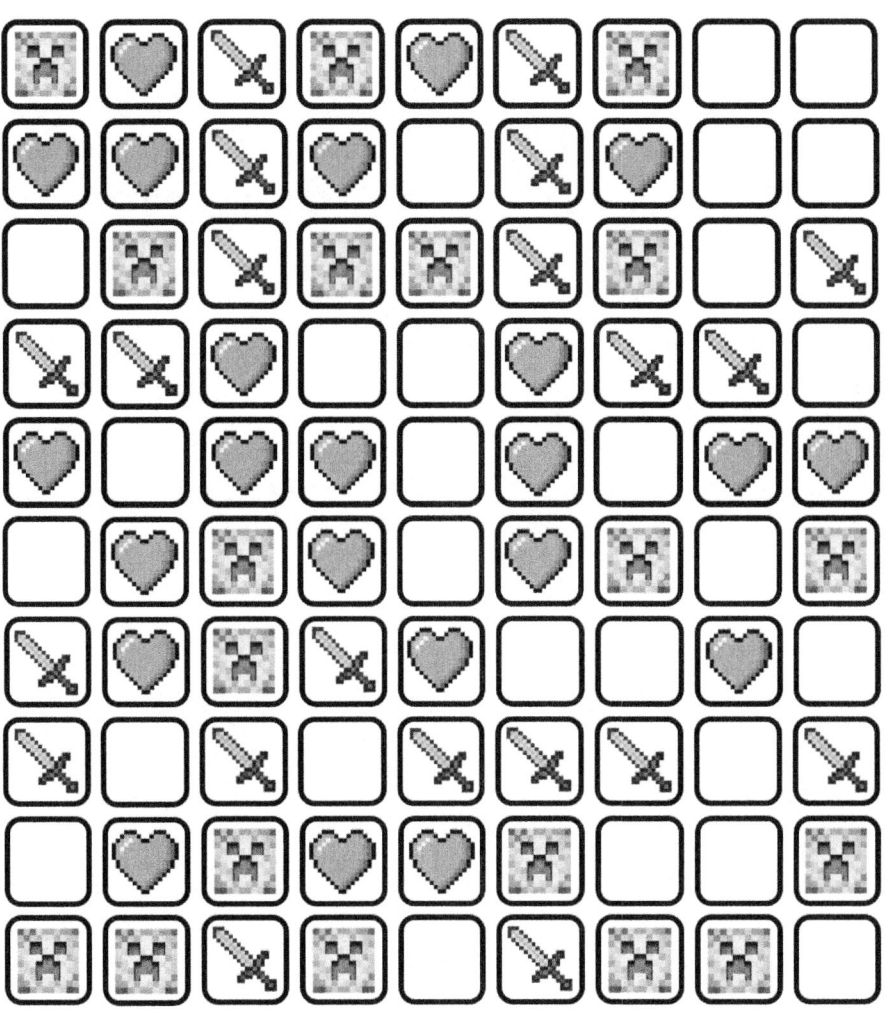

INTERMEDIATE • SQUARE NUMBERS

THE DOLPHIN'S CHEST

Each of the dolphins leads us to a secret chest that contains the result of its operation. There is one dolphin that doesn't lead to any chest. Which one is it?

Answer: _____

Chests: 36, 16, 64, 81

Peter 7^2

Jane 4^2

Mary 9^2

Jack 8^2

Steve 6^2

INTERMEDIATE | PROBLEM SOLVING

DIVIDE AND CONQUER

Large slime creatures split into smaller ones when attacked, and so on, until they become small slime balls. In the drawing below, you can see how the slime creatures divide.

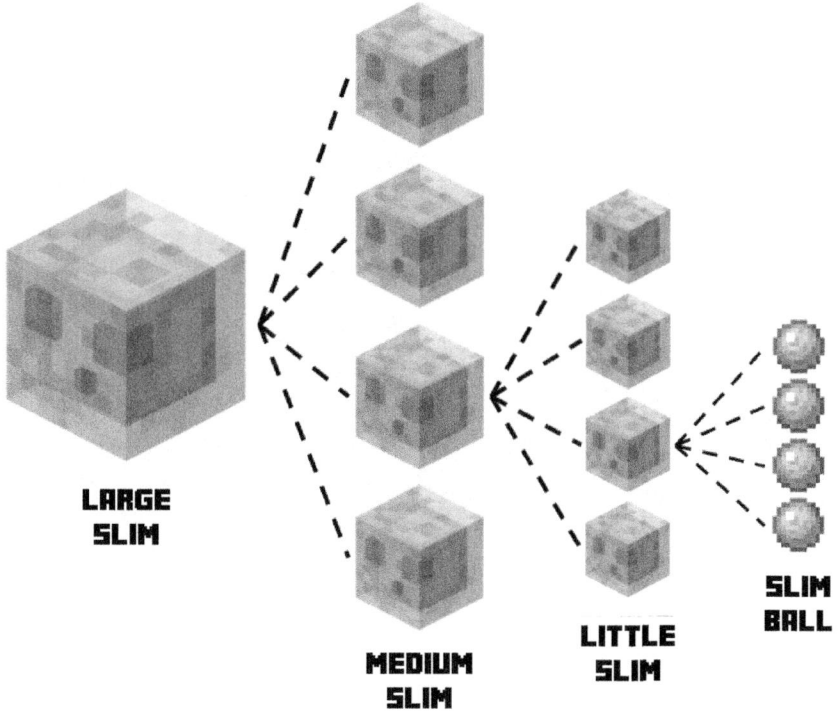

LARGE SLIM

MEDIUM SLIM

LITTLE SLIM

SLIM BALL

1. While exploring a swamp, Alex encounters 2 large slime creatures. After fighting and defeating them, they turn into balls. How many balls has Alex obtained in total?

Answer: _____

2. When Steve defeats a large slime, he receives 6 experience points, and 3 points for each medium slime. Steve finds 3 large slimes in a cavern, which he eliminates, turning them into balls. How many experience points does he earn in total?

Answer: _____

INTERMEDIATE ‖ **PROPORTIONALITY**

TASKS OF THE DAY

In the following cube, all the tasks that Steve performs in a day over 24 hours are represented. Considering the space each task occupies, complete the hours Steve dedicates to each one.

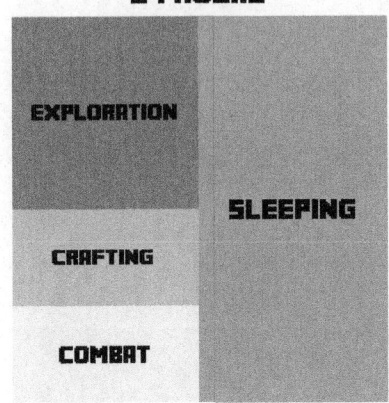

NUM. HOURS	
SLEEPING	
EXPLORATION	
CRAFTING	
COMBAT	

MY OWN CASTLE

We need to help calculate the amount of each material that Alex used to build his own castle. Alex remembers that the materials he used the most were stone and brick, and he used the same amount of both. In addition, he used twice as much wood as glass. Look at the chart below and, using Alex's hints, complete the number of blocks for each material.

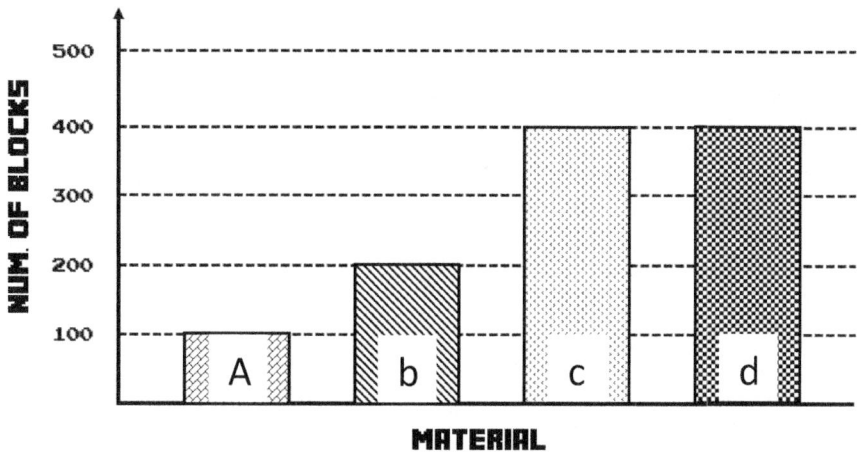

1. Stone: _____   2. Brick: _____

3. Wood: _____   4. Glass: _____

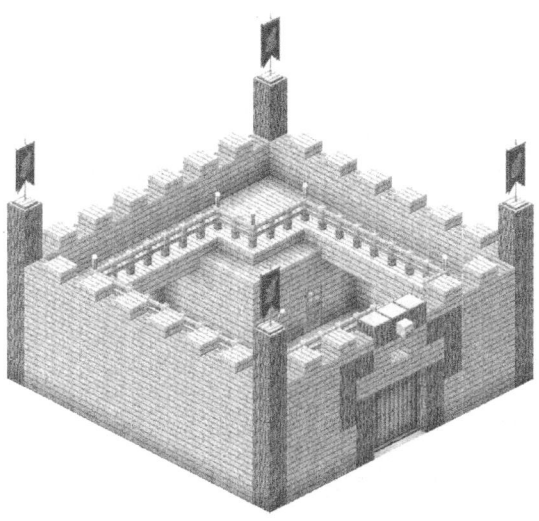

THE PASSAGE OF TIME

The table below shows the relationship between real time and the time that elapses within the Minecraft world.

REAL TIME	MINECRAFT GAME TIME
1 SECOND	1 MINUTE AND 12 SECONDS
1 MINUTE	1 HOUR AND 12 MINUTES
1 HOUR	3 DAYS
1 DAY	2.4 MONTHS

1. On Monday morning, Oscar played for 5 minutes before having breakfast and going to school. How many hours in the Minecraft world does that time correspond to?

    Answer: _____

2. If 24 complete days have passed in the Minecraft game, how much real time has Oscar spent?

    Answer: _____

3. During the vacation months, Oscar played a total of 10 days. How many years in the Minecraft world does all that time correspond to?

    Answer: _____

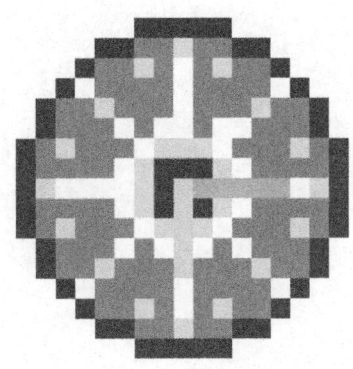

ADVANCED LEVEL

ADVANCED ⋅ AREA AND PERIMETER

TOM'S LITTLE HOUSE

1. Tom's little house is shaped like a rectangle. We know that the area of the house is 20 blocks, and the perimeter is 18 blocks. What are the length and width of the house?

Answer: _____

2. Tom has built a stone fence in a rectangular shape around the entire house. The fence measures 24 blocks in length and 16 in width. On one of the sides, 2 blocks have been removed to build a door. What is the perimeter of the fence excluding the space for the door?

Answer: _____

3. Tom wants to farm near his house and is preparing his own garden with cultivated soil blocks. The garden is rectangular with a total of 50 soil blocks. We know that the length of the garden is double its width. What are the dimensions of Tom's garden?

Answer: _____

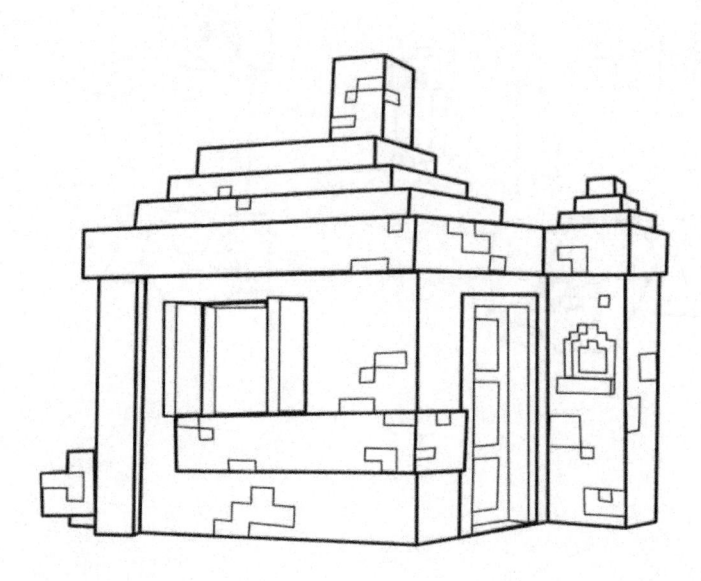

ADVANCED :: PROPORTIONALITY

FOOD BANK

Stacy is very generous and has decided to donate a part of the produce from his gardens to the food bank, so that the less fortunate villagers with scarce resources can eat.

- For every 4 pumpkins he harvests, he donates 1 to the food bank.

- For every 20 carrots he harvests, he donates 8 to the food bank.

- For every 7 blocks of sugar cane he harvests, he donates 3 to the food bank.

When the harvest is complete, Stacy has a count of 36 pumpkins, 200 carrots, and 63 blocks of sugar cane. Write below each figure the number of units that Stacy must take to the food bank.

1. Pumpkins:_____    2. Sugar cane:_____

3. Carrots:_____

ADVANCED ∥ **AREA AND PERIMETER**

THE VEGETABLE GARDEN OF MAYRA

Mayra has planted carrots, wheat, pumpkins, and melons. Follow the clues to guess what she has planted in each of the following gardens. Write the name inside the garden.

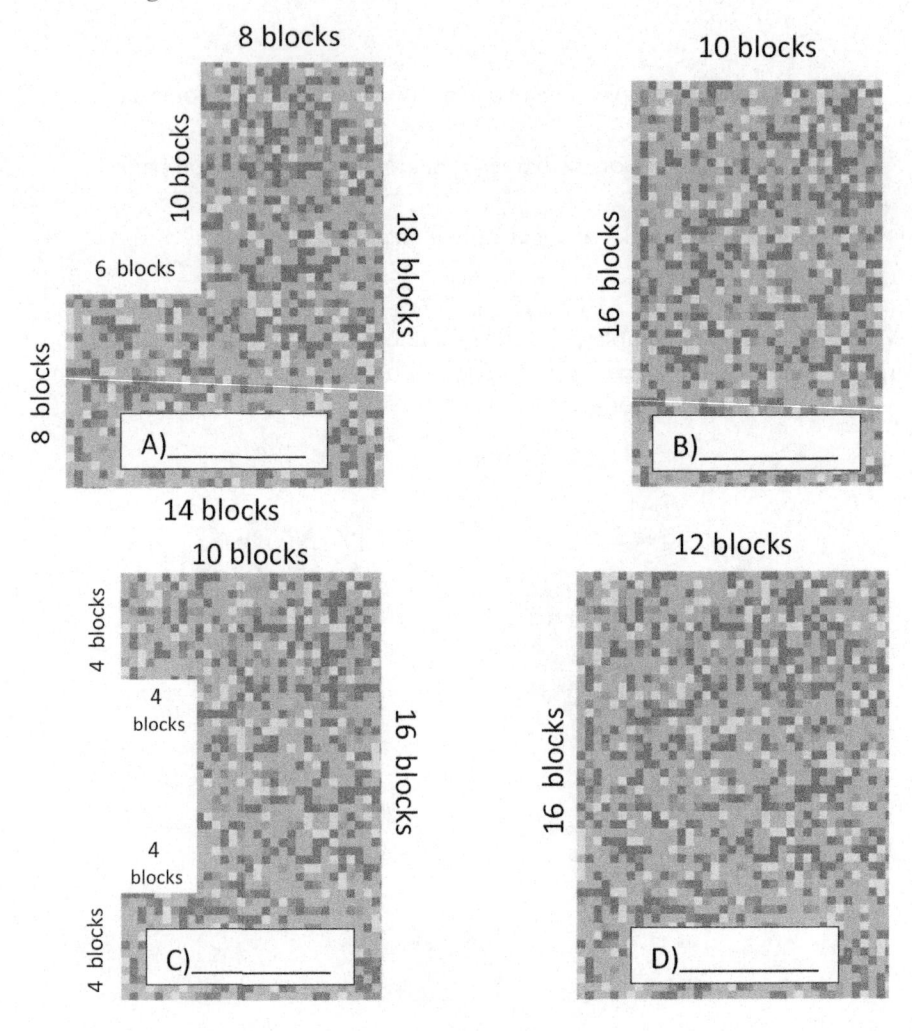

8 blocks

10 blocks

6 blocks

18 blocks

8 blocks

A) _____

10 blocks

16 blocks

B) _____

14 blocks

10 blocks

4 blocks

4 blocks

16 blocks

4 blocks

4 blocks

C) _____

12 blocks

16 blocks

16 blocks

D) _____

- The area of the carrot garden is equal to that of the melon garden; however, the perimeter of the melon garden is greater.
- The area of the wheat is double that of the perimeter of the melon garden.

40

ADVANCED II DATA HANDLING AND PERCENTAJE

COUNTING ANIMALS

Steve has a farm with a total of 1200 animals. We need to help him fill in the table below to find out how many animals of each type there are. Use the following information to complete the table:

- Half of all the animals are sheep.
- 30% of the sheep are babies.
- The small pigs are half the number of baby sheep.
- The number of adult pigs is 20 units more than the baby pigs.
- The number of baby chickens is the same as that of baby pigs.
- The number of adult chickens is three times that of the baby chickens.
- The number of adult cows is a third of the number of baby chickens.
- There are three times as many adult cows as there are baby cows.

Hints to check if you have done it correctly:

- The total number of baby animals is 370.
- The total number of adult animals is 830.

	BABY Animals	ADULT Animals
Pigs		
Chickens		
Cows		
Sheeps		

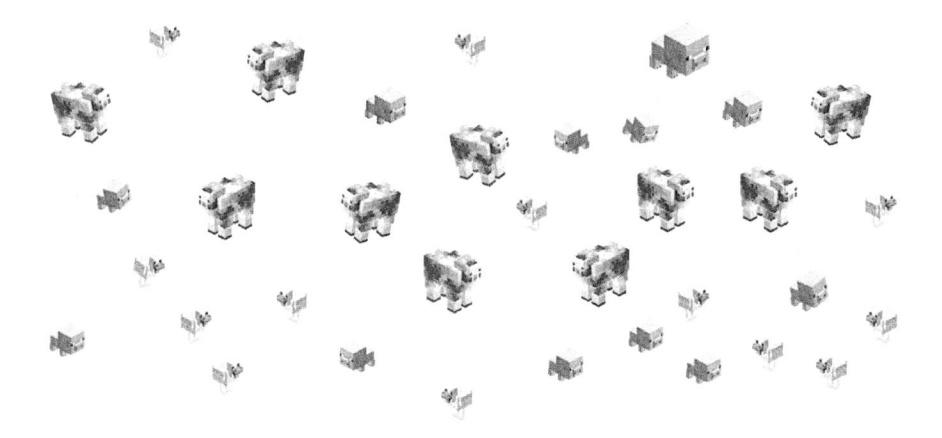

ADVANCED | PROBLEM SOLVING

FALSE REDSTONE

One of the torches doesn't light up because it is connected to a redstone block that is false. The following clues tell us which blocks are true and therefore light up their corresponding torch:

- The blocks that are multiples of 3 light up the torches.
- The blocks that have a square number light up the torches.
- The blocks that have a prime number light up the torches.

Which torch remains unlit? Answer: _____

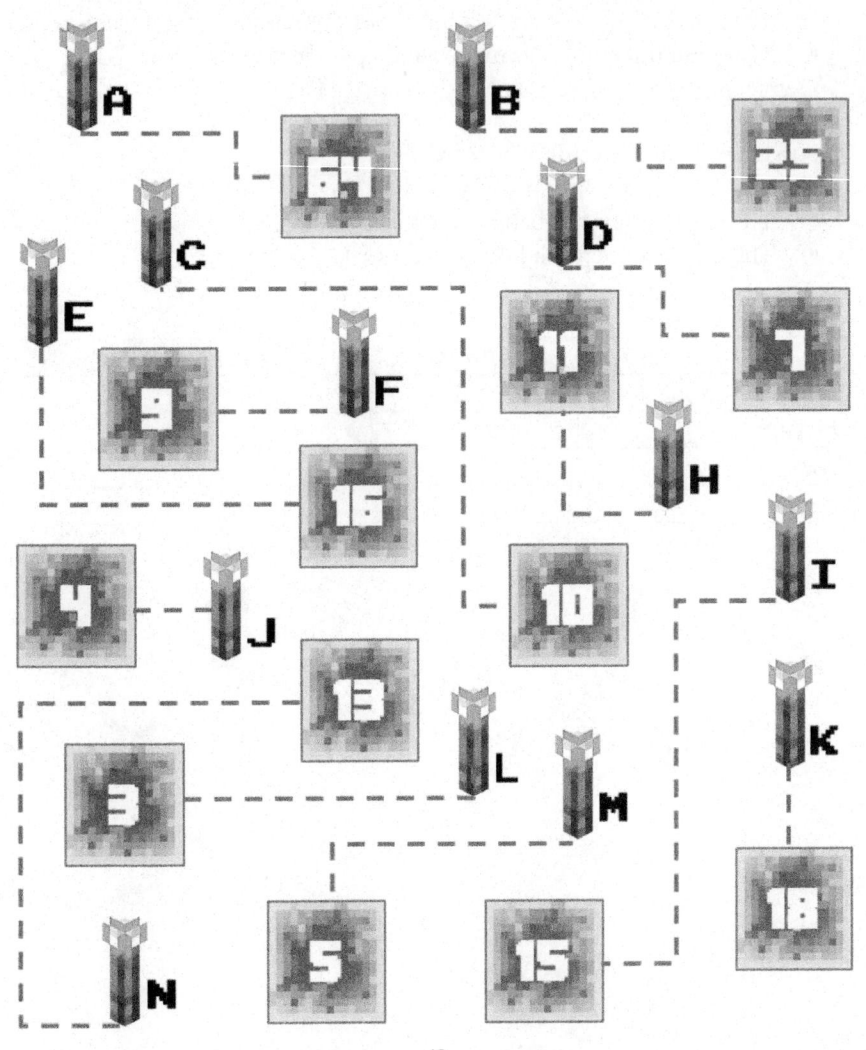

ADVANCED ⅠⅠ DIVISION. PERCENTAJE

WATERING LANDS

One water block is capable of watering 4 blocks of soil around it; therefore, with 1 water block, 80 blocks of soil can be irrigated.

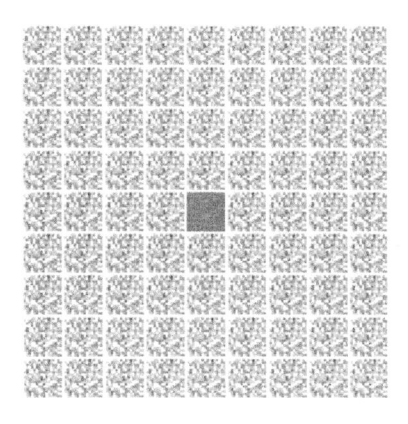

DIRT

WATER

1. How many water blocks are needed to irrigate 1200 soil blocks?

Answer: _____

2. The field in the image below has a water block in one of its corners. What percentage of the total remains unwatered?

Answer: _____

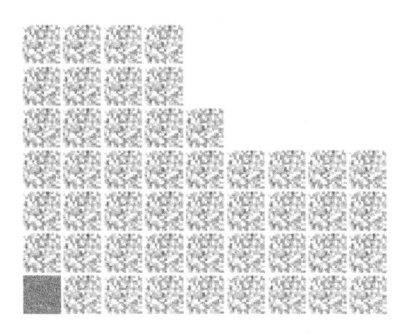

ADVANCED | PERCENTAJE PROPORTIONALITY

THE SPIDERS ATTACK

1. When a spider dies, the probability of dropping 2 strings of rope is one fourth (1/4). How many strings of rope could Alex collect if he defeats 220 spiders?

   Answer: _____

2. Sometimes spiders spawn with a skeleton on top. The probability of this happening is 1%. How many skeletons would appear if 300 spiders are spawned?

   Answer: _____

3. In the latest beta version of Minecraft, there is a golden spider that has a one-third (1/3) chance of dropping a magic potion when it dies. We also know that 50% of the magic potions are poisonous. If Steve eliminates 24 golden spiders, how many poisonous magic potions could we collect?

   Answer: _____

ADVANCED || DATA HANDLING. PERCENTAJE

ALEX THE ARCHITECT

Alex is planning the construction of his next house and for this, he has prepared an inventory with the following materials and quantities of blocks.

MATERIAL	NUM. OF BLOCKS
STONE	750
TERRACOTTA	200
BRICKS	150
OBSIDIAN	140
REDSTONE	110
WOOD	80
GLASS	70

1. What is the total number of blocks that Alex is going to use to build his new house?

   Answer: _____

2. What material makes up 50% of the house?

   Answer: _____

3. What percentage does the brick represent with respect to the total number of blocks in the house?

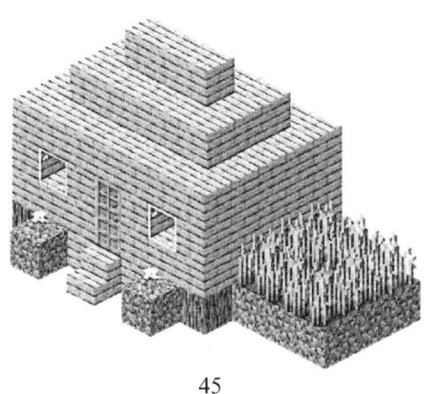

   Answer: _____

SOLUTIONS
BASIC LEVEL

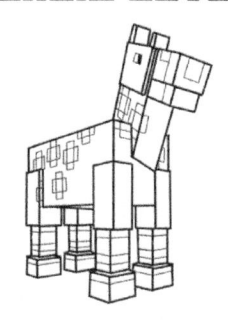

THE ISLAND OF MUSHROOMS

1) 7 red mushrooms
2) 7 soup
3) 9 hunger points

ALEX'S NEW ARMOUR

1) 25 emeralds
2) 1 emerald

COUNTING BLOCKS

1) 7 blocks
2) 27 blocks
3) 31 blocks
4) 19 blocks
5) 69 blocks

STEVE HAS A SWEET TOOTH

1) 7 cakes
2) 3 cakes
3) 10 cakes in the even-numbered boxes (2 and 4)
4) 17 cakes in all the boxes

BLOCKS SEQUENCE

1) 2, 4, 6, 8, 10, 12, 14, 16, 18, 20, 22, 24, 26, 28
2) 6, 9, 12, 15, 18, 21, 24, 27, 30, 33, 36, 39, 42, 45

SOLUTIONS
BASIC LEVEL

FLOWER BOUQUETS

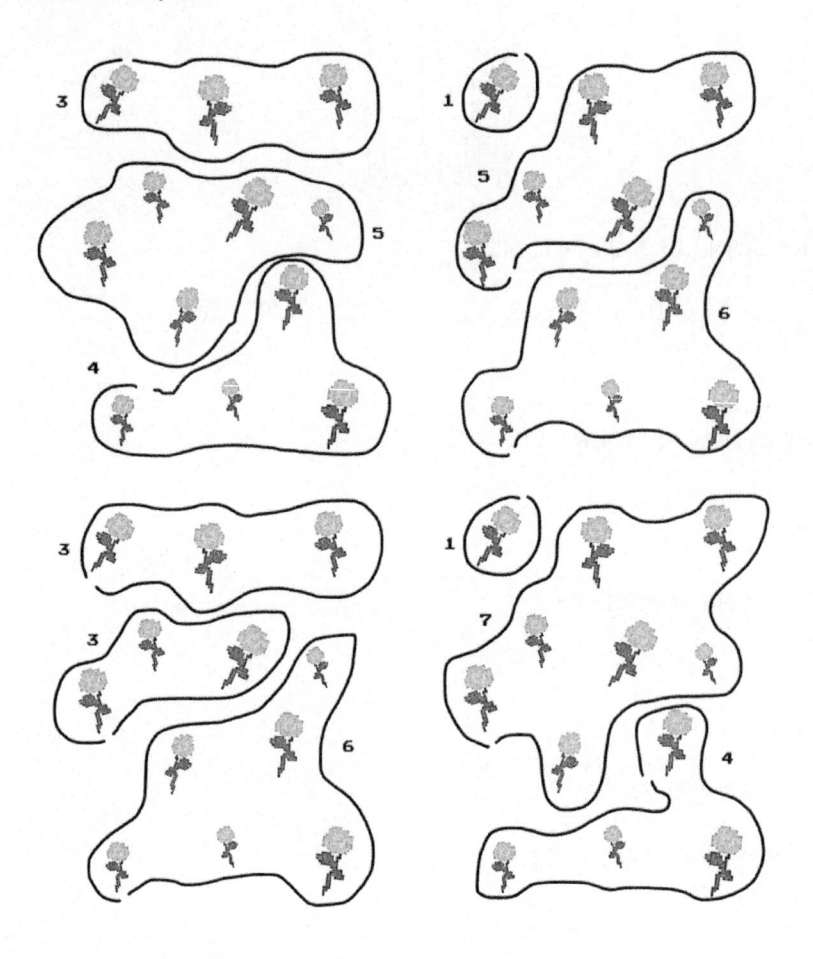

CREEPERS ATTACK

1) 6 creeper

SOLUTIONS
BASIC LEVEL

COUNTING MY LITTLE ANIMALS

1) 15 chickens
2) 10 donkeys
3) 55 (25 pigs + 20 horses + 10 donkeys)
4) 70

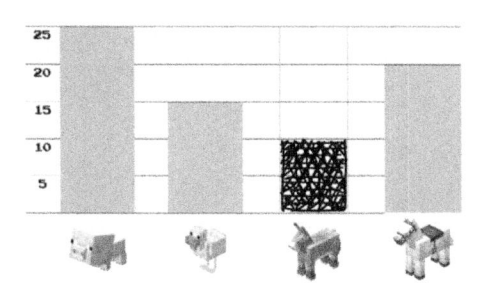

CARROT HARVEST

1) Wednesday
2) 14 carrots (4 Tuesday + 2 Wednesday + 7 Thursday)
3) 26 carrots (Total)
4) 5 carrots (7 Thursday – 2 Wednesday)

BITCOIN MINE

1) 25

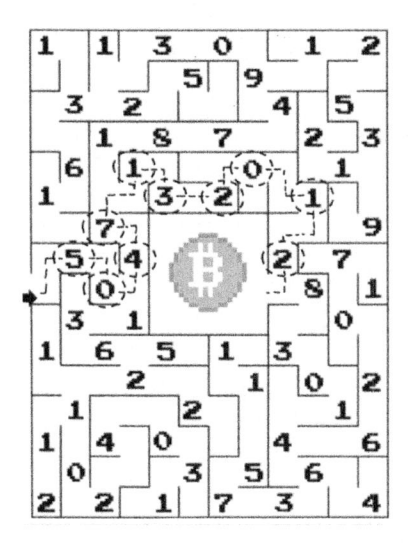

SOLUTIONS
BASIC LEVEL

MASTER ARMORER

1) 1 shovel and 1 pickaxe (7 emeralds + 11 emeralds = 18)
2) 1 axe, 1 shovel and 1 hoe (22 emeralds)

COORDINATES X Y

1) Pickaxe (5,2)
2) Pig (1,4)
3) Chicken (6,4)
4) TNT (4,5)
5) Emerald (3,3)
6) Chestplate (2,1)

SECRET CODE

1) Cookie
2) Bread
3) Meat
4) Fish

DEACTIVATING TNT

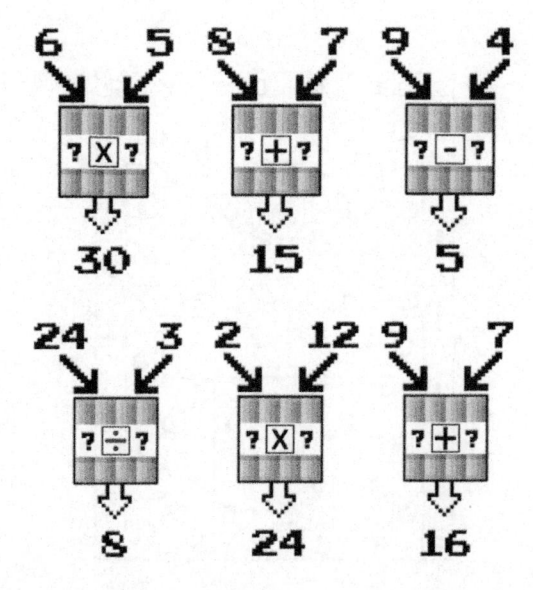

6 × 5 = 30
8 + 7 = 15
9 − 4 = 5
24 ÷ 3 = 8
2 × 12 = 24
9 + 7 = 16

SOLUTIONS
INTERMEDIATE LEVEL

OCELOTS IN THE JUNGLE

1) 10 raw cods
2) 9 ocelots
3) 1 raw cod
4) 3 creepers

THE OCELOT'S LIFE

1) 45 ocelots
2) 20 ocelots
3) 30 ocelots
4) 64 chickens

BLACK SHEEP

1) 8 sheep
2) 8 health points
3) 24 blocks

CRAFTING WITH IRON

1) 8 helmets
2) 5 chestplates
3) 10 boots
4) 5 chainmails

THE DAY'S SCHEDULE

1) Farming
2) Farming
3) Melting
4) 3 hours (180 minutes)

SOLUTIONS
INTERMEDIATE LEVEL

ACTIVITY	START HOUR	END HOUR	DURATION
MINING	07:00 A.M	07:30 A.M	30 MIN
FARMING	07:30 A.M	07:50 A.M	20 MIN
MELTING	07:50 A.M	08:40 A.M	50 MIN
CRAFTING	08:40 A.M	09:15 A.M	35 MIN
COMBAT	09:15 A.M	10:00 A.M	45 MIN

WHEAT, BREAD AND COOCKIES

1) 81 wheat spikes
2) 40 cookies (10 wheat spikes spent)
3) 23 pieces of bread (69 spikes)
4) 2 spikes left

BREAD AND FISH

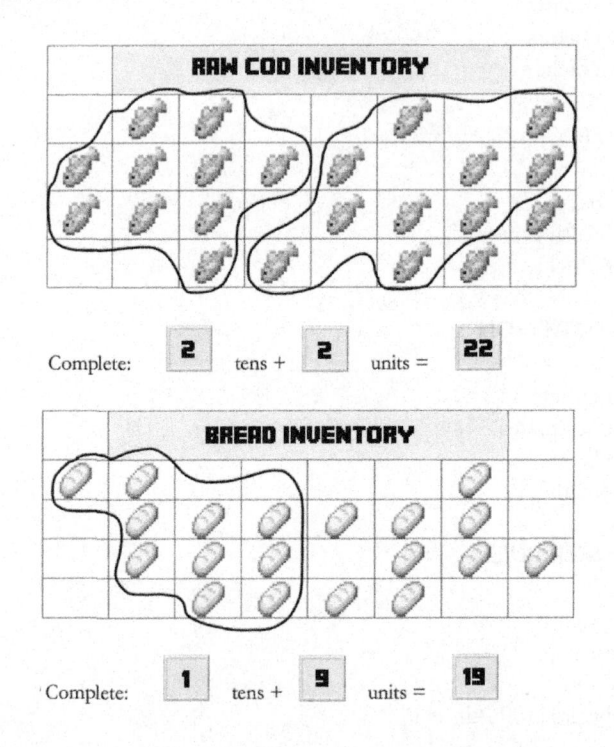

RAW COD INVENTORY

Complete: **2** tens + **2** units = **22**

BREAD INVENTORY

Complete: **1** tens + **9** units = **19**

SOLUTIONS
INTERMEDIATE LEVEL

BLOCKS SEQUENCE V2

SOLUTIONS
INTERMEDIATE LEVEL

THE DOLPHYN'S CHEST

1) Peter (49)

DIVIDE AND CONQUER

1) 128 balls
2) 54 experience points

TASKS OF THE DAY

	NUM. HOURS
SLEEPING	12
EXPLORATION	6
CRAFTING	3
COMBAT	3

MY OWN CASTLE

1) Stone: 400
2) Brick: 400
3) Wood: 200
4) Glass: 100

THE PASSAGE OF TIME

1) 6 hours. Minecraft time
2) 8 hours. Real time
3) 2 years. Minecraft time

SOLUTIONS
ADVANCED LEVEL

TOM'S LITTLE HOUSE

1) 5 blocks (length), 4 blocks (width)
2) 78 blocks (24 + 24 + 16 + 16) – 2
3) 10 blocks (length), 5 blocks (width)

FOOD BANK

1) 9 pumpkins
2) 27 sugar cane
3) 80 carrots

THE VEGETABLE GARDEN

a) Melon
b) Pumpkins
c) Wheat
d) Carrots

COUNTING ANIMALS

	BABY Animals	ADULT Animals
Pigs	90	110
Chickens	90	270
Cows	10	30
Sheeps	80	420

SOLUTIONS
ADVANCED LEVEL

FALSE REDSTONE

a) Torch C. (Number 10)

WATERING LANDS

1) 15 blocks
2) 50%

THE SPIDERS ATTACK

1) 110 strings of rope
2) 3 skeletons
3) 4 magic potions

ALEX THE ARCHITECT

1) 1500 blocks
2) Stone
3) 10%

Printed in Great Britain
by Amazon